Original title:
Where the Hallway Leads

Copyright © 2025 Creative Arts Management OÜ
All rights reserved.

Author: Elliot Harrison
ISBN HARDBACK: 978-1-80587-101-9
ISBN PAPERBACK: 978-1-80587-571-0

Secrets of the Passageway

A door creaks open with a smile,
Inside lies a sock, not seen in a while.
Dust bunnies dance in a cheerful parade,
Whispering secrets the vacuum has laid.

Mice play chess with crumbs as their prize,
While the cat in the corner rolls its wise eyes.
Every step reveals a wiggle and shake,
What wonders await? Let's venture and take!

Through the Dim Light

A flickering bulb casts shadows so strange,
Catch a glimpse of a poster, slightly deranged.
Ghosts of forgotten pizzas float by,
With splatters of sauce just making you sigh.

Old shoes with stories are lined on a rack,
Each sole a tale, ready to crack.
Wanderers giggle, they tumble and trip,
In the dim light, let imagination flip!

Trails of Creativity

Crayons paint dreams, some wild, some bright,
As paper airplanes take off in flight.
Markers march like soldiers in line,
While glue sticks giggle, feeling so fine.

A treasure map drawn on a lunchbox lid,
Leads to a missing homework bid.
Chasing ideas, we skip and we spin,
The fun's in the journey; let's begin!

Stairways to the Imagination

Up we go on the wobbly stairs,
Where laughter echoes like wild dares.
Each step a bounce, a jump, a cheer,
We reach for the clouds, for those dreams so dear.

At the top, a wizard brews soup in a pot,
Full of strange veggies, it's tasted, why not?
The view is amazing; we giggle and sway,
Up here, the silliness rules the day!

The Weight of Silence

In the hush of night, shoes squeak,
A shadow jumps, I barely peek.
Cats strike poses, all quite grand,
Yet in silence, the world had planned.

Fingers itch to make a sound,
But the walls seem to wear a frown.
A tumble here, a knock there too,
Watch out for the chair; it bites you!

Who hid my keys? Oh, what a jest,
Maybe they're off on a secret quest.
Laughter echoes, taps of feet,
All this noise? It's quite the treat.

So I tiptoe on this floor,
Whispers "shh," but I crave more.
With every step, the creaks align,
Making silence a funny line.

Flickering Flames in Passage

Through the dim light, shadows dance,
A flicker, a jump, in a trance.
Candles burn with sassy flair,
While I trip on that darned chair.

Laughter warms the chilly air,
As ghosts join in with a flair.
"Did you see that crazy cat?"
It leapt so high, oh, what of that?

Tails are swishing, giggles rise,
In this hallway, fun supplies.
Bumps and thumps, a startled shout,
"Who turned the lights on?" "Not me, doubt!"

Yet still we shuffle, a happy band,
Chasing shadows, oh, isn't it grand?
With every stumble, a knock on wood,
I think this passage is up to no good.

The Veil of Mystery

Through veils of dust, a tale unfolds,
Whispers of laughter, secrets bold.
In shadows thick, a riddle spins,
What's in there? Let the fun begin!

Maybe a monster; maybe a mouse,
Peeking out from the corner of the house.
Under the bed, with socks in tow,
Someone's hiding; oh, who would know?

Tickles await in this cozy gloom,
Maybe it's just my vacuum's broom.
With every creak, adventures swirl,
In this strange world, watch the pearls twirl!

Unravel the yarn of silent mirth,
And chase the silliness of our birth.
Why take it serious? Let's just play,
In this mystery, we'll find the way.

Intricacies of the Journey

Oh, the twists and turns of fate,
With every bend, we celebrate.
Scooting through with glee, take care,
Watch that corner; it's a snare!

Maps are useless, laughs are found,
Just follow the squeaks of the ground.
Every echo tells a joke,
In this journey, let's provoke.

Muddy shoes and giggles galore,
Each stumble opens a new door.
So here we are, trek on with cheer,
In this maze, we've naught to fear!

With friends so dear, we run and shout,
In laughter's grip, we twist about.
Ah, the intricacies of the roam,
This silly path feels like home!

The Swaying of Distant Echoes

In shadows tall, I trip and stomp,
The echoes laugh, I feel the pomp.
They tell me tales of fun events,
As I sway on through their pretense.

A cat in socks slides by so slick,
I join the dance, it's quite the trick.
With every giggle, walls do sway,
Time to boogie, hip-hip-hooray!

The corners whisper, 'Take your turn',
I'll twirl and whirl, it's my big yearn.
A rug unveils its hidden art,
A symphony of clumsy heart.

A door creaks wide, I start to run,
Just where I land could be pure fun.
So buckle up, my feet prepare,
The journey leads to laughter's lair.

Canvas of Treaded Journey

With sneakers bright, I paint the floor,
Each tread a mark, the world's a chore.
I slide and glide like I own the place,
But trip on air, what a strange grace!

A painting laughs, it winks with glee,
I chat with it, 'Listen to me!'
The colors swirl, and I feel bold,
A masterpiece of stories told.

Around each turn, a mystery waits,
A newly painted line creates,
A backdrop for my wacky play,
Where every mishap's like a ballet.

I hop and skip, the brush in hand,
Creating chaos in this land.
Oh, what a canvas I have spun,
A gallery of giggles—what fun!

Beyond the Familiar Veil

Beyond the door, I hear a sound,
A ruckus brimming all around.
With cautious steps, I peek inside,
A surprise party—joy can't hide!

The cake's a mountain, frostings soar,
With every bite, I could explore.
But wait, a clown whips cream with flair,
And suddenly I'm in a chair!

The veil it parts, I'm tossed about,
In party hats, we dance and shout.
Though nothing's as it seems to be,
We laugh and spill in gleeful spree.

A slip and slide through pure delight,
The echoing laughter feels just right.
In every corner, fun does dwell,
Unraveling truths beyond the shell.

Threads of Destiny's Passage

With tangled yarn, I start to weave,
A tale of trips, I can't believe.
Each loop a step in playful schemes,
In threads of fate, I chase my dreams.

I tug and yank, the colors clash,
A squirrel peeks in, it's quite the splash.
We knit a story, wild and bright,
A tapestry of goofy sights.

A needle darts, it zips around,
I follow closely, lost but found.
We stitch together laughter's thread,
In knots and loops, we surf ahead.

At last we're done, the masterpiece,
Each silly pattern brings release.
With every thread, a giggle lingers,
In destiny's hands, we weave with fingers.

Passage to Possibility

A door creaks softly with a grin,
What chubby ghost is tucked within?
Sock puppets dance in wild delight,
As rubber chickens take to flight.

Down the path of mismatched shoes,
Where every choice comes with a snooze.
Chasing shadows that tell a joke,
And laughing fountains spray out smoke.

Unexpected friends in goofy hats,
Juggle donuts with acrobatic cats.
Join the party, you won't regret,
For silly surprises are the best bet.

So tiptoe through with glee and flair,
Adventure calls, so do beware!
For laughter waits around each bend,
In this hallway that has no end.

Veils of the Unexplored

What awaits behind that wobbly door?
A dance of ducks on a marble floor?
Silly whispers tickle the air,
While unicycles twirl without a care.

Beneath the surface, a bubble bath,
Filled with giggles and goofy math.
Counting fish that wear blue hats,
And juggling eggs with cackling chats.

An octopus with a cane so grand,
Leads the way with a wave of his hand.
Through fuzzy forests of candy trees,
Where popsicle birds sing melodies.

So push through curtains that shimmer and shake,
See what visions will make you quake.
Each step reveals a whimsical sight,
In a chamber that beams with delight.

Routes to Nowhere

The map is upside down, oh dear,
But follow the snail, he has no fear!
With a shell that's sprouting bubblegum,
He hums a tune that's quite the sum.

Around the corner, a cake parade,
With sprinkles flying, a wild charade.
Chasing after a rogue gummy bear,
Time flies fast when you don't care.

Invisible paths made of sticky tape,
Where jellybeans twist and bend like drape.
Every turn leads to a taffy fall,
And silly hatters that giggle and crawl.

So wander aimless, let laughter lead,
In endless loops of joy and speed.
For routes to nowhere are always fun,
When laughter echoes and time is done.

Mysterious Crossroads

Four signs point to a quirky fate,
With ice cream dreams that never wait.
One way leads to a fishy dance,
While another brings a flying romance.

Slippers that glow on the leading path,
Squeaky shoes that set you to laugh.
A unicorn wearing funky shades,
Joins the crew as humor cascades.

Turn left to find a garden of pies,
With juggling frogs and blue butterflies.
Or take the right to a library,
Where books come alive with hilarity.

So at these crossroads, take your best shot,
Embrace the silly, give it a thought.
Each choice blossoms with laughter and cheer,
In realms where joy is always near.

Map of the Uncharted Drift

A paper map that folds in three,
With drawings of a dancing bee,
It claims there's treasure past the door,
But all we found was upturned floor.

A compass points to nowhere fast,
It spins like it's a funhouse blast,
We trip on markers, laugh and shout,
In this adventure, there's no doubt!

We sailed on socks to distant lands,
With pillows as our steering bands,
The couch became our mighty ship,
Ignoring mom's brigade of grip.

So forward! To the fridge we roam,
In search of snacks we call our home,
With feasts of cereal loud and proud,
Our giggles echoed, cheers were loud!

The Lure of the Hidden Realm

Behind the curtains, tales unfold,
Of castles built and knights so bold,
Yet whispered hints of socks that smell,
Are woven deep in magic's spell.

We skulk and sneak in our disguise,
As kings and queens with daring eyes,
But shadows dance and giggles swell,
For cat's the fiend that guards our spell.

A wand is crafted from a straw,
With magic tricks that leave in awe,
We cast a spell to make lunch fly,
But all it does is make us cry!

Yet treasures lie in every nook,
Like mom's old dust and mismatched book,
Thus laughter leads our merry quest,
In realms of chaos, we're the best!

Illumination in the Gloom

In shadows thick, a glow appears,
A flashlight powered by our fears,
We chase the light; it flickers mad,
But darkness hides a playful lad.

Beneath the bed, a monster snores,
While plush toys guard the secret doors,
It's hard to tell who's brave or not,
When wiggly worms are all we've got!

We leap around in astronaut suits,
On quests to find the missing boots,
The dogs will tow us back to shore,
And we will plan a new galore!

We light the candles, share our dreams,
In laughter's grip, nothing redeems,
So here we'll sit, the giggles loom,
As echoes dance away the gloom.

Chasing Echoes Down the Lane

In search of echoes, off we run,
Through twists and turns, it's all for fun,
We call their names to hear them back,
But only find a silly quack!

With every step, the sounds grow bold,
A laughter caught in shades of gold,
We throw our voices, high and free,
While squirrels chase us up a tree.

Patrol the garden, spying foes,
With flowers that tickle our toes,
We dress the bushes for a show,
As garden gnomes join in the flow.

So if you hear a cheer today,
Know we're alive and here to play,
With echoes ringing through the lanes,
In silly songs, our joy remains!

Echoes of Unseen Doorways

In the corner, a cat stands proud,
Chasing shadows, feeling loud.
Is it a mouse, or just a sock?
Spooky tales, around the clock.

With every step, a creaky sound,
Who knew floors could be so round?
A ghostly laugh, a sudden trip,
Is this a dance, or a comic slip?

Behind the door, a feast awaits,
Leftovers from last week's debates.
A sandwich sings, a donut's grin,
What bonkers madness lurks within?

The echoes call, "Come join the fun!"
A treasure map, or just a bun?
In this maze, I've lost my way,
But laughter's here, I'll surely stay.

Shadows of the Passageway

In the passage, faint and still,
Wiggly shadows start to thrill.
A broomstick races down the lane,
Oh, what a sight—just pure insane!

A rubber duck, a wig, a shoe,
What this place has seen, who knew?
With every twist, the corners bend,
A wild journey with no end.

An echo yells, "Don't take a peek!"
But silly me, I'm far too cheeky.
What's behind that door so bright?
A puppet show or a food fight?

Laughter drips from every wall,
A masterpiece of pure absurdity's call.
When shadows dance, come take a chance,
Here mischief reigns, let's join the dance!

Whispers in the Corridor

Whispers swirl like leaves in air,
Playful secrets everywhere.
"Did you hear what jumped the fence?"
A frog in tights? A wild suspense!

A suitcase snores beneath the bed,
Is it alive or just misled?
Jellybeans spill like coins of fate,
Taste them quick, they might be late!

With each swift step, the walls confide,
"Here's a treasure you can't abide."
An octopus with squeaky charm,
Oh, don't you see it means no harm?

The corridor's alive with cheer,
Finding giggles lurking near.
So follow whispers, chase the fun,
In this madness, we have won!

Beneath the Flickering Lights

Beneath the lights that flash and dart,
A dance floor made of strobe and art.
Bizarre moves from an old man's jig,
Grab your partner—do a gig!

The lights go out, all's silent wide,
Enter a troll who wants to hide.
"Have you seen my shoes?" he cries,
Underneath the bed, where laughter lies.

Pirate hats and feather boas,
Surprise parties shape the ethos.
Under the glow, it's pure delight,
Join the chaos, it feels so right!

With every flicker, dreams appear,
An ever-changing atmosphere.
Step into giggles, jump and spin,
Who knew the fun was tucked within?

The End of Curiosity

I ventured down the corridor,
I found a door that squeaked and snored.
Inside, a cat with a monocle grinned,
He spoke of cheese, my courage thinned.

A dog in a bow tie danced around,
I lost my shoe, it fell to the ground.
The walls were painted with jelly beans,
A candy land of hilarious scenes.

I tried to escape but got trapped in a maze,
With marshmallow walls, in a sugary haze.
The cat winked twice, my heart raced fast,
Curiosity? It ran out at last!

So now I sit in a sticky delight,
Wishing my travels took me to the right.
Next time I'll stick to the straight and narrow,
Or just take snacks, like a clever sparrow.

Haunting Instincts

In a hallway dim, shadows danced,
I thought I'd found a ghostly chance.
But it turned out to be a clever mime,
Pretending to haunt, just killing time.

I chased the specter down the lane,
Tripped on my feet, fell back again.
He giggled up under his faux-white sheet,
And offered me pizza, it looked like a treat.

I laughed and asked for his ghostly tricks,
He juggled air, made me do kicks.
The specter said, 'Boo!' but I burst out in cheer,
Turns out ghosts just want fun and beer!

So amidst the laughter, I took a bow,
Haunting instincts? I'll leave those now.
For with every scream, there's laughter in store,
And who knew ghosts were so full of rapport?

Silhouettes in Twilight

Under the glow of a fading light,
Silhouettes danced in sheer delight.
A giraffe in a tutu? Yeah, that's the scene,
Twisting and twirling, quite the routine.

An elephant trumpeted, 'Join me, please!'
With a wink and a laugh, he tickled my knees.
We wobbled through shadows, no care in our steps,
This was the party, no one gets prepped.

As darkness fell, a raccoon in a hat,
Composed a sonnet about a fat cat.
The audience roared, what a sight to behold,
Turning twilight tales into legends untold.

So with every silhouette that came into view,
I declared, 'This is fun, not for the few!'
Let's dance our worries far, far away,
And dream silly dreams where we can stay.

Elysian Walks

I took a stroll on a path with flair,
Dancing daisies had quite the affair.
They spun and twirled in a floral ballet,
I chuckled aloud, joined in the play.

A squirrel named Ted offered me tea,
He poured with precision, oh can't you see?
With each sip, my troubles took flight,
While Ted recited poems, oh what a delight!

We chatted with owls about pizza pies,
They hooted with glee, quite the cheerful guys.
Each step was a giggle, the sun set low,
On Elysian walks, time skipped like a toe.

So if you feel down, just follow my lead,
Find your own path, let laughter impede.
For in every corner of jovial cheer,
Life's a funny story, so let's all revere!

Ghostly Footfalls

Creaking boards and whispered laughs,
A poltergeist with goofy gaffs.
It shuffles here and wobbles there,
In search of snacks and comfy chairs.

With every step, it trips and spins,
A phantom lost in silly grins.
It tries to dance but missteps stark,
And crashes down—the whole hall's a lark!

Echoes of laughter fill the air,
As ghostly pranks cause quite the scare.
But through the fright, there's humor found,
For laughter lingers all around.

In this place of haunting fun,
Where shadows play and ghostly run.
Join in the dance, embrace the call,
For who could resist this crazy hall?

Pathways of the Heart

In the maze of love, we stroll and stray,
Each twist and turn leads us to play.
With laughter as our guide so bright,
We skip through corridors, pure delight.

Every corner hides a silly tale,
From cheeky winks to a clumsy flail.
Our feet trip over passion's spark,
As we navigate this quirky park.

A door swings open, and out flies a kite,
Chasing dreams on a whim of light.
With a giggle, we chase, we dart,
In the pathway where humor imparts.

Let's dance through these wild, vibrant halls,
With heartbeats echoing joyful calls.
In this whimsical journey, let's play our part,
Embracing the laughter that fills the heart.

Unspoken Journeys

There's a path where silence speaks,
With hidden paths and playful leaks.
Why whisper secrets in the shade?
When giggles bloom, let fun invade!

With sock puppets tripping on the floor,
And rubber ducks that proudly soar.
Each leap we take, a comic feat,
In this less-traveled lane, we meet.

So let us prance, let's twirl and glide,
On pathways where our chuckles ride.
The tapestries of laughter weave,
Adventures waiting to believe.

We may not share each silly thought,
But every giggle says a lot.
On this journey, together we start,
With joy, my friend, let's cartwheel our heart!

Reflections on the Wall

On the wall, my face appears,
With goofy smiles and silly sneers.
It laughs back with cheeky delight,
Encouraging a dance in the night.

A glance away, a wink, a nod,
In this mirage, I'm quite the prod.
The frame's too tight for all my charm,
But the laughter keeps me free from harm.

Sometimes it mocks, with quirky stares,
As I pratfall down the winding stairs.
In this hall of fun, what will I find,
But silly silliness that's truly kind.

So let's embrace the funny sight,
Let's dance with joy, hold on tight.
For in this hall where laughter thrives,
The wall reflects our merry lives!

Portals to the Past

A door swings wide, I take a peek,
Inside there's a dragon playing hide and seek.
Old socks and gadgets from days of yore,
They giggle and dance, begging for more.

A knight with armor that's better days,
Tries to do the cha-cha in curious ways.
With teacups and snickers from ancient brew,
Every moment's a laugh, who knew?

I step back twice and hear a tune,
A raccoon wearing glasses, a paper moon.
He winks at me, says, 'Let's take a ride!'
We zoom through the past, with nothing to hide.

I laugh as I tumble through epochs of cheer,
Finding my lunch from the last thousand years.
Time bends and twists, a curious art,
Who knew history could be such a lark?

Chasing the Unfamiliar

A shadow whispers, 'Come and play!'
I stumble and trip, in a most awkward way.
Chasing a ghost with a wobbly grin,
It beckons me on, where could it have been?

Through alleyways grinning with neon lights,
Each twist and turn gives comical sights.
A cat with a monocle reads the news,
While shoes do the tango, in colorful hues.

I meet a creature, all fuzzy and round,
It bubbles with laughter, a sound profound.
Together we dance on this peculiar street,
Through portals of hilarity, life's neat!

I chase the unfamiliars, they lead me astray,
But who would decline such a whimsical day?
With laughter as currency and smiles all around,
I'm richer than ever; what joy I have found!

Landscapes Beneath Our Feet

Look down, oh friend, at the pavement's grin,
It plots and schemes as I step in.
Cracks are the lines of ancient maps,
Leading to treasures, where giggles collapse.

A gumdrop forest grows from the street,
Where candy canes sprout from beneath my feet.
The pavement hums a silly old tune,
As squirrels in top hats dance 'round a moon.

Beneath my soles, the world takes flight,
With puzzles aplenty, oh what a sight!
Each step's a giggle, a laugh, a cheer,
These landscapes of nonsense draw me near.

I leap over puddles that splash with glee,
As rubber ducks flutter, oh come, look and see.
The ground tells stories, a comic embrace,
In every funny footfall, I find my place.

Through the Mist of Time

Through vapors of giggles, I wander and roam,
Each step takes me on a journey back home.
Silly specters jump from the streams of the past,
With cackles of laughter, they're free at last.

A jester takes flight on a broomstick with flair,
Offering marshmallows to lighten the air.
A time-traveling toaster pops up with toast,
While I laugh and savor what I love the most.

I trip on an hourglass, it spills like sand,
On the floor are old jokes from a whimsical band.
Each grain is a chuckle, each tick of a clock,
Turns moments to memories wrapped in a sock.

Through ridiculous whispers, I skip on the breeze,
Past moments of joy that grow roots like trees.
The mist of the ages tickles my side,
In a funny parade where fun does abide!

The Doorway's Secret

Behind the door, there's quite a tale,
A dancing cat, a moose in scale.
With socks on hands, they all did play,
In a world where night outshines the day.

Each knob a riddle, each hinge a jest,
They laugh so loud, you'd never rest.
A chair that spins, a hat that sings,
Such nonsense, oh, the joy it brings!

A mirror speaks with a wobbly tongue,
Telling tales of old when life was young.
It made me giggle till my sides did ache,
In this hall of fun, there's no mistake.

So open wide and take a peek,
Adventure waits for those not meek.
In every corner, a surprise gleams,
In a doorway filled with splendid dreams!

Steps into Silence

Upon the steps, a band of shoes,
Whisper secrets, share their views.
One shoe says, 'I need a dance!'
While others sigh, 'We missed our chance!'

A boot debates with a worn-out flip,
The elegance of style and grip.
'Let's head outside!' the sandals cry,
But here we are, in silence, why?

The carpet rolls its eyes with glee,
As dust bunnies laugh, 'Oh, let it be!'
They dart around, in hasty flight,
While we decide to argue polite.

It's quite the scene, this still tableau,
Where footsteps falter, yet laughter flows.
In every echo, a joy divine,
If silence speaks, it sure sings fine!

Avenues of Memory

Through avenues paved with laughs and cheer,
Old toys chatter as I draw near.
A teddy bear tells tales of the past,
While trains whoosh by, quite unsurpassed.

A kite once lost, now flies on cue,
In dreams we shared, just me and you.
Old photos giggle from the frame,
Recalling moments that we can't tame.

My slippers stomp with a purposeful beat,
As I roam down lanes of wobbly feet.
Remembering picnics, splashes, and splats,
In the echoes of silliness, we tip our hats.

So here I stroll, through jests and song,
In the lanes of laughter, I still belong.
Each turn a chuckle, every glance a grin,
In the avenues where memories spin!

The Labyrinth of Thought

In the maze of gray, my brain takes flight,
A squirrel races, oh, what a sight!
Around the corners, I trip and bounce,
In a puzzle where rabbits seem to pounce.

Doodles dance on every wall,
A monkey swings, I hear its call.
'Forget the plan, let's play a game!'
In this labyrinth, nothing's the same.

A thought pops up like a grand parade,
With confetti made of dreams displayed.
But oh dear me, where is my shoe?
In this maze of brain, I feel brand new!

So round and round, to nowhere we go,
In a world of giggles, just letting flow.
The labyrinth may twist, but here's the score,
With every zany turn, who wants more?

Fractured Realities

In a place where socks conspire,
Lost in some unseen shire.
My shoes have gone for coffee,
And my keys? They laugh, so lofty.

The mirror winks with a grin,
Spaghetti monsters pull me in.
I chase my shadow down the lane,
And bump my head on thoughts insane.

An umbrella dreams of flight,
While I pretend I'm a knight.
The doorbell sings a silly tune,
As I question the day, too soon.

With puddles that giggle and sigh,
I wave at clouds drifting by.
The clock is playing hide and seek,
And I'm just here, feeling quite weak.

A Glimpse Beyond

Through a crack in my old door,
A cat with a cape did soar.
It winked at me, full of flair,
As I wondered how on earth it got there.

A table dances with glee,
While chairs gossip joyfully.
Cups are knitting fuzzy hats,
Saucers laugh like chubby rats.

The wall suggests I take a peek,
At the fridge that starts to speak.
It says, 'Your leftovers are neat!'
And I chuckle at the strange treat.

In this world of quirky sights,
I trip over the softest lights.
With each heartbeat, laughter's close,
What a wild, funny dose!

Impressions in the Dust

Footprints lead to nowhere fast,
In a world that's built to last.
Dust bunnies dance upon the floor,
As I watch them tease the door.

Each swirl holds a playful shout,
With moments I can laugh about.
Tables laugh beneath the sun,
They told me dust can't be fun!

The wall clocks tick in silly ways,
Counting all my funniest days.
Sketches come alive and prank,
With giggles echoing, I quietly thank.

In the corners, secrets play,
With shadows teasing night and day.
The vacuum's plotting its next tale,
While I sit back and just exhale.

Circles of Wander

Round and round, I spin and sway,
Chasing thoughts that go astray.
The ceiling fan waves at me,
While I question it's all a spree.

With each step, I lose my way,
A map made of silly clay.
The fridge hums a catchy beat,
As I dance – oh, what a feat!

Balcony cats cheer my stunts,
While pillows join the funny fronts.
Every wall is a new surprise,
Where even the picture frame sighs.

In endless loops of cheerful fun,
Laughing until the day is done.
I follow a path of giggles sweet,
With memories that can't be beat.

Footprints on Dusty Floors

In a house of laughter and surprise,
Footprints dance, oh what a guise!
They lead to cookies, crumbs do spill,
Chasing shadows, what a thrill!

Each step a secret, a giggle reveals,
A trail of mischief, oh how it feels!
Mom's looking puzzled, dad's in a huff,
But look at the footprints, they're just too tough!

Mismatched socks, a mystery game,
Each wiggle brings the same old fame!
From here to there, we make our mark,
With muddy shoes, we'll leave a spark!

So if you find a wandering shoe,
Just know it's not me, but my crew!
For in this house, fun never ends,
With footprints and giggles, our laughter blends!

The Illusion of Infinite Paths

Down the corridor, paths so bright,
Where each corner twists out of sight!
One way leads to a shoe by the door,
Another leads to snacks galore!

I took a left, then darted right,
Met a cat dressed as a knight!
He said, 'Good luck on your quest, dear friend,'
But told me the snacks were his to defend!

Oh, choices galore, what shall I choose?
To chase after snacks or a cat in blues?
So many paths, it makes me grin,
Should I take a leap or just spin?

These twists and turns, a jolly maze,
I float through life in a lovely daze!
With laughter echoing, I'm on my way,
To endless snacks or a cat's ballet!

Riddles of the Untraveled Route

In a place where echoes play a tune,
Lies a riddle hidden, a sweet cartoon.
Is that a door? Or merely a wall?
To knock or to listen, oh what a call!

Around the bend, a voice does sing,
'What is the sound of a dancing spring?'
I scratch my head, with a grin so wide,
Maybe it's just my socks that slide!

Up ahead, a sign with arrows askew,
'Choose your path, just don't lose a shoe!'
Do I follow the wind or the scent of pie?
I'd take the pie, no need to ask why!

So here I wander, a traveler's spree,
With riddles unfurling, wild and free!
Each step a mystery, each laugh a cheer,
In this untraveled route, I have no fear!

Crossroads at Midnight

At midnight, all the paths collide,
With glowing signs and ghoulish pride!
'Choose your destiny!' the wisps all shout,
But really, they're just playing about!

The first path promises lots of cake,
The second, a dance with a rubber snake!
I hesitate, then start to laugh,
Why not try both? Take a crazy path!

A ghostly figure with a wink and nod,
Points to the cake and gives a prod!
But then the snake, it starts to sway,
I'll have my cake, but dance all day!

So in this crossroads, I make my stand,
With a bite of cake and snake in hand!
For at midnight, there's funny delight,
In each silly choice, I find pure light!

In the Silence Between Steps

In a stretch where footfalls linger,
I found a sock, a lone singer.
It chirped a tune, quite absurd,
and danced around like a silly bird.

Beneath the light, a shadow pranced,
but it slipped away, a missed chance.
With every creak, the floorboard sighed,
as if it knew secrets it tried to hide.

A broomstick waved, and dust flicked high,
a laugh escaped, it felt so spry.
As I twirled in this quirky show,
a chair laughed too, "Oh, take it slow!"

In the silence, magic blooms,
in forgotten corners or dusty rooms.
As laughter echoes off the wall,
one sock beckons - it's a free-for-all!

Through Veils of Time and Space

Through bends and twists of whimsical air,
I stumbled upon a peculiar hair.
It belonged to a cat, or was it a llama?
Either way, it stirred up drama.

In the second stall, a cactus spoke,
"Don't touch my spines; I'm not a joke!"
Yet, as I giggled, it wobbled some more,
and rattled off tales of a wild, wild bore.

So I paused to listen to its tale of woe,
a dance with squirrels in a striking glow.
Every step I took, space shifted and swayed,
as if the universe decided to play.

I tripped over laughter, bounced off the wall,
a cosmic giggle, an interstellar ball.
Past time and logic, I'd lost track of hours,
all while being rained on by confetti of flowers.

The Hidden Portal's Call

Behind the picture, a portal gleamed,
a door to a land where reality steamed.
Unicorns lounged while teapots swirled,
and jellybeans sparkled, an odd world unfurled.

A penguin in boots offered me tea,
he said, "Come on in! You'll be least bored with me!"
I thought for a moment, then took a chance,
but tripped on a rug, and began to dance.

The walls were alive, with laughter so loud,
even the ceiling seemed somewhat proud.
Each sock and shoe had stories to tell,
yet I kept on stepping, under their spell.

I curtsied to ducks and bowed to a cat,
at every turn, a new friend to chat.
In this hidden place, I wandered far,
where mischief sparkled like a shooting star.

Unraveled by the Unknown

Step by step, my path unwound,
into a realm where quirks abound.
My shoes began to giggle and leap,
while the doorway creaked in laughter deep.

Hints of magic clung to the air,
as I passed a ghost with curly hair.
It tickled my nose, and I let out a sneeze,
which sent the curtains swaying like trees.

A clown on a tricycle chased after me,
squeezing balloons, so purposely.
He said with a grin, "Join in the fun!
a world without limits has just begun!"

So I let loose, joined the fray,
a dance of silliness, come what may.
In a daze of laughter, I twirled and spun,
in a realm where every day's a pun!

Solitary Steps

One foot in front, the other unsure,
A dance with my slippers, I'm destined for more.
I shuffle and slide, I trip on my shoe,
The cat rolls her eyes; she knows what I do.

A mirror reflects my outlandish retreat,
With socks of two colors that never compete.
I step on a toy, and oh what a screech!
The hallway's a stage, and I'm here for a speech.

I pray for a snack that's just out of reach,
The fridge, oh sweet fridge, hear my loyal beseech!
But when I arrive, it's an empty cold shelf,
And I only find veggies—I'll blame it on self.

A circle I make, from room to the hall,
Chasing my dreams, or maybe a ball?
Each corner I turn's like a joke in disguise,
In this labyrinth of laughter, I find my surprise.

The Unfolding Trail

Step by step on this winding path,
Each bend I encounter provoked by a laugh.
I stammer and giggle in my own silly way,
As the shadows behind me engage in play.

With walls that seem whisper secrets untold,
And paintings that grin at the stories of old.
A door creaks open, I stumble and fall,
Now I'm face first in a well-placed faux wall.

The puppy runs past me, his tail up in glee,
Chasing after fragments of pure, wondrous spree.
I join in the wild, forgetting all grace,
On this unfolding trail, I'm sent into space!

The final surprise waits at the end of the lane,
A box full of treasures, but all are in vain.
With all of my dreams wrapped up nice in a bow,
But all that I find is just an old toe.

Radiant Echoes

In the hallway of mirth, echoes bounce off the wall,
A melody chirps, in a whimsical call.
Here all my thoughts dance in synchronicity,
While the slippers do tap with a joyous decree.

The shadows stretch long, just avoiding my feet,
As if they're aware of my raucous defeat.
A shadow leads laughter with each step that I take,
Mixing up all of my moves like a jumbled-up cake.

I twirl like a leaf, lost in the breeze,
With echoes returning as symphonic teas.
A chorus of chuckles, I follow the sounds,
In this carnival hallway, pure weirdness abounds.

But wait—what's that? A snack on the floor!
Exploring my world, I discover a score.
I pause to indulge on this mystical treat,
Only to find it's a crumb! Very neat.

Receding Shadows

As I tiptoe along with no destination,
The shadows behind me craft a great narration.
They dance with such flair, they twirl to and fro,
As I guess what's hidden in their playful show.

But wait! Is that a comedy? Oh, what a sight,
My footsteps are staccato in their rush of delight.
A glance in the mirror shows me quite clumsy,
With hair tousled wildly, looking most funny.

The hallway stretches far—an endless buffet,
With options for mischief that brighten the gray.
The vacuum awaits with its loud, bumpy tune,
And I'm headed straight for it, like a fool to a rune.

A tumble, a wiggle, and there goes my shoe,
Rolling away, looking back, who knew?
With echoes of laughter like music at play,
These receding shadows will guide my stay.

Doors to the Infinite Maybe

A door creaked open, what might be found?
A sock, a shoe, a cat lying round.
Do I want snacks, or a quest for gold?
Who knows what awaits in this hallway so bold?

I flip a coin, a fateful spin,
To follow a trail of a runaway grin.
Left for lasagna, right for a rant,
Maybe I'll get both, but probably can't!

Through mirrors and shadows, I dance with flair,
What lies beyond? An old teddy bear?
He's judging my choices, giving me sass,
I'll bribe him with jellybeans—oh, what a class!

A door slams shut, it mutters a note,
"Next time, dear friend, just stick to the boat."
But who needs a boat in a hall of surprise?
I'll take the next step; let's see if I rise!

The Unwritten Path of Hearts

In a hallway of choices, I stall with a glance,
A dance with the walls? I'll take the chance.
What if the left is a party galore?
And the right is a nap? Oh, I do implore!

A sign reads, "Go back," but not on my clock,
I'll bravely proceed, dressed as a rock.
The scent of popcorn floats up from below,
Or is that just me? I do not quite know!

A heartbeat in laughter, a giggle in flight,
Found a balloon dog, what a strange sight!
He wags and he wobbles, he's cheerful and bright,
Inviting me over to join in his plight.

Unwritten, unwritten, this path feels so free,
With spaghetti dreams and a key made of glee.
So here in this hallway, I dance with delight,
An unwritten journey, oh what a fright!

Melodies of the Wandering Soul

In the hallway's murmur, a tune starts to hum,
It tickles my ears, oh, isn't it fun?
Maybe a polka or a funky old beat,
I trip on the mat with two left feet!

Each door that I pass sings a verse of its own,
One whispers of breakfast—'tis endless scone!
Another's a waltz with a marzipan bear,
Shaking paws and tails, who's got time to care?

A band of lost shoes joins in the parade,
With rhythm and rhyme, an anthem is made.
Do I lead or follow? The question is clear:
With melodies swirling, I'll dance without fear!

As the hallway winks with a twinkle and spin,
I laugh at my choices; oh, let the fun begin!
For life's just a song, let it roll and unfold,
In this merry corridor, adventures untold!

Light at the Far End

A glimmering shimmer beckons me near,
Is it freedom, or maybe a giant smear?
A light bulb flickers; the ceiling does hum,
Could it be dinner or just a big drum?

I tiptoe ahead, with my nose to the glow,
Do I smell pizza? Oh boy, let's go!
But what if it's monsters, waiting for treats?
I'll face them with laughter and too many sweets!

The light shifts and dances, a kaleidoscope tale,
Cinco de Mayo with a side of wail.
It's bright and it's bold, like a carnival fair,
With popcorn and laughter, who could dare?

At the end of this journey, a prize awaits me,
A seat by the fire, a soft comfy spree.
So out of the shadows, into the light
I dine on fun dreams and hold on tight!

Hidden Entrances

In a room filled with shadows, I looked for a door,
Found a cat in a hat, with a penchant for lore.
He winked and he smiled, asked if I could stay,
For a party of mice was set up for today.

Behind the wardrobe, a pirate ship sways,
With squirrels as crew, they laugh in their ways.
I hopped on a plank, feeling quite bold,
"Join us for treasure," the squirrel said, "gold!"

An attic with secrets, it seems never ends.
Even Grandma joins in with her paper mache friends.
We sailed to the kitchen, discovering pies,
Oh, the adventures found in the most silly lies!

As the light turns to night, the giggles grow loud,
In our vast little world, I'm feeling quite proud.
With doors that lead nowhere, and windows so wide,
Who knew where I'd end up? I'm happy inside!

Footprints of Solitude

There's a path in my house where I often stray,
It's traveled by slippers, always in play.
Each step that I take leaves a mark of delight,
But the dog has an issue, he chews on my light!

I followed the tracks to the hall's end unknown,
Where shoes whispered secrets and socks felt alone.
One said, "Let's dance!" in a jig by the wall,
While slippers made rhymes, their laughter a sprawl.

A curtain that twinkled with stars up above,
Said, "Look at these footprints of friendship and love."
But the vacuum came roaring, it took off the fun,
And the socks rolled in fear, "Oh no! We must run!"

In the end, it's a journey through laughter and scorn,
With no map or compass, just shoes that have worn.
Sometimes solitude hums a quirky old tune,
With ghosts of my slippers, and that cat with a moon.

Light and Shadow Interplay

In the dance of the day, shadows stretch like a cat,
Mimicking shapes of my favorite old hat.
Light chuckles and giggles, hides 'round the bend,
While shadow plays tricks, like an old sneaky friend.

A bunny hops close, casting shapes on the floor,
While sunlight bursts in, through the cracks of the door.
They argued and bantered, in a flickering spree,
"Catch me if you can!" said the light with a glee.

The clock on the wall chimed an hour absurd,
Echoes of laughter drifted on every word.
With each little flicker, the shadows would prance,
Creating a world where all things could dance.

As twilight rolled in, it painted a sight,
With colors that mixed in a playful delight.
So here in this lounge, the shadows hold sway,
While the light keeps on laughing at this funny play!

The Space Between

In the space that I found, just a crack in the wall,
Lived a family of ants who were having a ball.
They invited me over to join in their fun,
Said, "We dance through the sugar when the day's done!"

With a sprinkle of laughter and grains here and there,
They served up sweet stories, like it just didn't care.
Their queen wore a crown made of crumbs and some fluff,

"If life gets too tough, just munch a bit of stuff!"

But just down the street, in the neighbor's home,
Lived a sneaky old cat who would try to comb.
With a flick of her tail, she interrupted the scene,
Said, "You can't have your fun—this is solely my routine!"

Yet the ants just giggled, with crumbs on their cheeks,
"We're family of mischief, and laughter's our peaks!"
In the space that I found, tucked away with delight,
Life is just sweeter when it's filled with a bite!

Puzzles of the Path

A door slams shut, the lights go dim,
I found a cat, but it's not a whim.
The floorboards creak, they giggle with glee,
A map in my hand, but it's just a tree.

I trip on a rug, it's soft and so blue,
The ghost tells jokes, who knew ghosts could do?
Chasing old shadows, they laugh and they twirl,
I swear that lamp just gave me a whirl.

Invisible walls, I bump with a thud,
A sock on the wall gave me quite a crud.
What's round is a corner, what's up is the floor,
I'm quite sure this path has a pop-up door!

Laughter echoes loud, it falls from the sky,
With every right turn, I just can't comply.
In a maze made of giggles, I'm lost in a bind,
But who needs to find it? I actually don't mind!

Threads of the Unraveled

A knitted cocoon, I pull on a thread,
It unravels quickly, can't keep up my dread.
A fork in the fabric, I go left then right,
A llama appears, dressed up for a fight.

The walls start to spin, I'm caught in a whorl,
With wooly companions, I dance and I twirl.
Here's a cat in a hat, but wait, is it real?
He hops like a bunny; what's the deal, what's the deal?

The yarn starts to tangle, my thoughts play a game,
Each twist leads me back, but it's never the same.
A laughter of colors, they shimmer and slide,
In this tangled-up haven, there's nowhere to hide.

So let's sip some tea with our fiber friends near,
In this maze of the bizarre, there's nothing to fear.
With laughter as currency, we'll trade in delight,
For each puzzle forgotten, brings joy in the night.

A Realm of Ambiguity

In a land where the clouds wear polka dot hats,
And squirrels throw parties while juggling of bats.
I ask for directions, a frog gives a nod,
But did I request comedy? That's quite the facade!

The signs point in circles, they wink with a grin,
A hula-hooping octopus invites me to spin.
"Follow the rainbow!" it says with a cheer,
But I tripped over rainbows, fell flat on my rear.

A path lined with giggles, I tumble and roll,
Bouncing through laughter, that's how I stroll.
With whispers of wind that play tricks on my ears,
I'm dancing with shadows, consuming my fears.

This realm flips my thoughts like pancakes in air,
Every turn is a riddle, a whimsical snare.
Yet here in confusion, I find solace and zest,
In the jumbled-up journey, I've found I'm quite blessed!

Time Stopped

Tick-tock sings the clock, but it's frozen in place,
I moonwalk through minutes, a neoliberal space.
A penguin on roller skates joins in my jest,
Time opened its portals, but forgot I'm a guest.

I throw popcorn at seconds, they pop all around,
Each kernel a moment, that won't hit the ground.
With chocolate rivers flowing from a fountain of fun,
I'm dancing with seconds, we laugh till we're done.

A wobbly hourglass spills giggles like sand,
In this timeless terrain, it's all perfectly planned.
The clocks go bananas, with arms raised in glee,
Staying still is a party; come join me, you see!

So let's wade through this puddle of moments unspent,
With laughter our compass, we need not lament.
For in this stillness, we'll savor and dive,
In the joy of the now, we truly arrive!

Fragments of Tomorrow

In the corridor of dreams, I stray,
Chasing shadows that giggle away.
Each step echoes with laughter and cheer,
In places unknown, but somehow near.

I find doors marked 'Do Not Enter',
With signs of a party, but no one to center.
A dance with the dust and a waltz with the light,
As my shoes take their turns in a whimsical flight.

Old coats hang like ghosts on a rack,
Whispering secrets of things they can't track.
They nudge me to listen, to stay and to play,
But the next room holds cake—wait, I mustn't delay!

In this maze of delight, each corner I bend,
Leads to more laughter, like time I can spend.
I'll stroll through this funhouse, no end in sight,
In fragments of tomorrow, oh what a night!

Halls of Reflection

Mirrors line up in a dazzling array,
Each one contains something silly to say.
I wink at my twin, who just winks right back,
In this hall of reflections, we giggle, we snack.

Footsteps tap dance on polished wood floors,
Echoing jokes from behind little doors.
The walls have ears, and their laughter's contagious,
As I recount blunders, they're ever outrageous.

This place is a riddle wrapped in a jest,
Where pondering life feels like an uninvited guest.
Clowns in the corners have no sense of space,
Each chuckle a reminder of our goofy embrace.

So in this strange hall where fun never fades,
I'll linger awhile while my reflection parades.
With a grin on my face and a hop in my stride,
I'll dance with the mirrors—my silly side rides!

The Unseen Companion

Walking a path where shadows conspire,
I talk to the air, it never gets tired.
An unseen companion with whispers of fun,
It tickles my thoughts like rays from the sun.

We wander through places that twist and that turn,
In this playful chatter, there's always a burn.
Each step is a riddle, a giggle, a glee,
A mystery unfolding—just my friend and me.

It nudges my arm when I'm taking a chance,
Encouraging mischief in a quirky dance.
'Why not try that door?' it playfully chimes,
And I find myself laughing at nonsensical crimes.

So here we shall travel, through nonsense and jest,
My invisible buddy knows me best.
With laughter our compass, we'll always be bold,
In the corridors silly, with stories retold!

Maps of the Inward Journey

I pull out a map, but it's just scribbled lines,
Leading to nowhere, yet somehow it shines.
Each mark on the paper is filled with delight,
Charting my laughter under the moonlight.

There are circles and doodles, some arrows that twist,
A treasure of giggles—oh how could I miss?
I follow the paths where the whimsy has flowed,
Through tunnels of chuckles and secrets bestowed.

The 'X' that marks laughter, I stumble upon,
With jokes buried deep, like a treasure long gone.
Each step on this journey breeds nonsense anew,
Mapping the laughter, just me and my view.

In a world of my making, I'm free to explore,
As humor unravels, my spirit will soar.
With maps in hand, I'll navigate thought,
Finding joy in the laughter, that is all I sought!

Pages of the Unwritten

In a house with many doors,
I found a sock and three old floors.
With clowns and ducks so out of place,
These pages blank, a silly race.

Once a cat danced on a hat,
I tripped on my dog, imagine that!
Under the bed, a treasure map,
Marked with crumbs, and a small nap!

In a closet, I found a pie,
It whispered gently, 'Give me a try.'
With each turn more oddities blend,
A mystery that has no end!

So take a trip with no straight line,
Find the laughter buried in time.
With each twist and turn, you'll see,
Life's a joke, just laugh with glee!

The Last Turn

At the last bend in the hallway,
I found a llama who was at play.
It wore a hat and danced with flair,
While squirrels cheered from a tiny chair.

A grandfather clock ticked with glee,
A tap-dancing floor just wanted to be free.
I held my sides, the joy was grand,
With chocolate chips that seemed quite planned.

Through the twist there lay a slide,
My socks flew off, what a wild ride!
Suddenly, I was in a booth,
With a talking burger - oh, the truth!

Each turn ignites the strangest sight,
In the madcap world, what pure delight!
So take that turn and spin around,
In the absurd, joy can be found!

Marks on the Door

Marks on the door, what could they mean?
Zebra stripes or a pizza bean?
A tape measure spills from the frame,
With scribbles that dance to a cheeky game.

A duck with sneakers quacked a song,
In bright pink shades, it danced along.
Each scribble told tales, oh so wild,
Of a sock thief and a trouble-making child.

One mark is a map to a garden of fun,
Filled with flowers that tickle in sun.
A party of ants held a parade,
With a piñata that bursts, how they played!

So knock on the door, let the laughter flow,
These marks hold stories, let them show.
In each silly sketch, a world so bright,
Open the door, step into the light!

The Enigmatic Path

Down an odd path that twists and weaves,
I met a hedgehog wearing leaves.
It offered riddles, silly and sweet,
While a frog played drums with its webbed feet.

A squirrel held court with acorns galore,
While a rabbit opened a joke shop door.
Why did the chicken pursue the hare?
To compete in races, they made quite a pair!

Each step revealed a fruitcake tree,
With dancing cherries and a bumblebee.
The path was tangled, oh what a sight,
With giggles echoing, taking flight.

So wander the routes that whirl and spin,
In the realm of wonders, let the joy in.
With laughter as your guide, you'll find,
The mystique of this path is fun, unconfined!

A Journey Within the Walls.

In a space with walls so bright,
I tiptoe left, then dash to the right.
Behind a door, I hear a sneeze,
Did the cat just make me freeze?

A mirror tells me I look grand,
Yet there's a sock, who made this stand?
I twirl with pride, as I check my shoes,
Did I just lose? Oh, what a ruse!

I walk through shadows, take a peek,
Find stashed popcorn, "Oh wow, a treat!"
Is that my old hat on a shelf?
Maybe this place knows me so well.

With giggles echoing in the air,
I dash around with zero care.
Each corner hides a silly tale,
An adventure grand, lest I derail!

Paths Unseen

Longing for fun with every twist,
I spy a path that can't be missed.
Round the corner, a surprise awaits,
My shoelace trips me, oh the fates!

Across a threshold, what do I find?
A treasure chest, but oh so blind!
Full of memories and socks galore,
Laughter bubbles, who could ask for more?

A dance of dust bunnies in the air,
I join their jig without a care.
"Where to next?" I'm on a quest,
In this maze, I'm feeling blessed!

Suddenly I'm in a blanket fort,
With teddy bears, it's such a sport.
Inside this realm, we laugh and cheer,
Every hallway whispers, "Stay right here!"

Echoes of Wandering

Through whispers of walls, I softly creep,
Eager to see what secrets they keep.
An echo calls, "Check under the bed!"
I trip on a shoe, was that really said?

Around the bends, I chase my dreams,
Only to find my laundry seems.
It's a sock monster, it seems quite real,
The giggles and thrills are quite the deal!

A parade of shadows, they dance and sway,
Taunting me softly to come out and play.
With each silly turn, my heart takes flight,
Oh, the adventures in this odd light!

Listing all echoes of laughter and fun,
My journey's just begun, oh how I run!
Each chamber gleams with tales yet unsaid,
In the heart of this maze, I'll never dread!

Shadows of the Unknown

With a flick and a flutter, I peek inside,
At shadows that whisper, "Come on, let's glide!"
They dance on the walls with a cheeky flair,
Turning the mundane to wonder so rare.

A broomstick zips by, let's take it for a spin,
Did it just wink? I guess it's a win!
We'll brew the giggles, the laughs and the fun,
In this light-hearted riddle, we've only begun.

Chasing the shadows through turns and bends,
Hopping on giggles, my laughter ascends.
Every corner beckons with curious might,
In this joyful maze, all feels just right.

With a map made of smiles, I traverse each nook,
Every creak of the floorboards fills me with good luck.
There's magic in mystery, joy stitched with thread,
In a realm unforeseen, I gladly tread!

Forks in the Dark

When shadows dance and giggles grow,
My feet are lost, but where to go?
A left, a right, oh what a mess,
I trip on laughter, what a jest!

A mirror laughs, it grins so wide,
It makes me question who's inside.
A snack or snack-less, which to choose?
In dark corners, I just can't lose!

I hear a voice, it calls my name,
The sock on my foot, it plays a game.
With every twist, a giggle bears,
In all this darkness, joy ensnares!

So bring your snacks and join me too,
In this maze of giggles, we'll break through!
To fork or not, that is the art,
In this fun realm, let's never part!

Uncharted Footsteps

Each step I take, a crunch I hear,
A pathway waits, it's full of cheer.
With every tap, a new surprise,
Oh look! A shoelace lies in disguise!

To the left, there's a splat, oh dear,
I think I've stepped on yesterday's cheer.
With every twist, giggles gather,
As I dance through the hall like a mad hatter!

The wall's a Meryl, it cracks a smile,
A friendly ghost, let's stay a while.
Footsteps echo with playful cheer,
Who knew a hall could feel so near?

Adventure calls in every stride,
With funny tales I'll never hide.
So join this dance, don't fear the fall,
In uncharted footsteps, we'll have a ball!

Ghosts in the Hall

What's that sound? A giggle shrieks!
A ghostly tale from wooden creeks.
With sheets and chains, they strut with glee,
Booing softly, come dance with me!

In every corner, whispers spin,
A hairy toe or wiggly pin?
They claim to haunt with charm and grace,
But really, it's just a playful race!

One drags a cat that wails in fright,
A snooze-worthy ghost, oh what a sight!
In sheets draped high, they tell their joke,
A phantom slapstick, purest bloke!

So if you hear a silly squeal,
Don't run away, it's part of the deal.
Embrace the fun, this ghostly thrall,
For laughter echoes down the hall!

The Edge of Tomorrow

Peeking out beyond today,
What lurks there, come out to play?
A future bright, a bag of tricks,
With silly hats and goofy licks!

A time machine, with wheels and flair,
Zooming past without a care.
I'll twist the knobs, see where it lands,
In naps and snacks, let's make some plans!

What's that? A pie from yesteryear,
Filling the air with laughter and cheer.
In tomorrow's world, it's all a jest,
With every twist, I'm surely blessed!

So pack your dreams for this wild ride,
Where giggles dwell and smiles glide.
The edge of time, a jump and shout,
In fun tomorrow, we'll figure out!

Secrets of the Wandering Path

In shadows thick, the whispers leap,
With socks unmatched, we take a peep.
A cat in boots, it struts with flair,
Off to a party, but we're unaware.

Old doors creak, with a grumpy moan,
Spinning tales of some long-lost bone.
Bouncing echoes, the laughter spills,
Who's hiding there? Just Mr. Thrills!

Chasing dust bunnies in a mad parade,
Along the walls, where colors fade.
The windows giggle, in brief delight,
As we stumble on into the night.

Mysteries swirl like a playful breeze,
Stepping boldly, with wobbly knees.
Lurking behind a quirky chair,
Invisible friends—do they really care?

Fragments of Forgotten Journeys

Footsteps echo, where no one goes,
Past the fridge that whispers prose.
With sticky notes and silly clues,
I find the sock that you might lose.

Here's a map, but it's upside-down,
Leading to treasure? Or just a frown?
Jellybeans sprinkle the carpet trail,
As we trip on stories, strange and pale.

A plush llama guards the crafted door,
In its eyes, adventure does soar.
Each twist and turn, a moment of glee,
A quest for the lost remote? Maybe three!

Yet laughter lingers through every nook,
In each hidden corner, there's a book.
So let's toast to journeys of wacky delight,
With whimsical tales that dance in the night.

The Labyrinth of Dreams

A hallway bends like a rubber band,
Where socks turn to ninjas, oh so grand!
Fridges hum tunes as we skip and hop,
Searching for snacks, we'll never stop.

Peeking through doors with a noodle-laced grin,
Finding a kingdom where jellybeans win.
A dragon? No, just a snoring cat,
In a pirate hat, and a polka-dot spat!

Tangled threads of the night unwind,
As echoes tickle the back of the mind.
We'll swing on a chandelier made of fun,
In a world where all logic is undone.

So twirl around in this kaleidoscope,
With bubbles of laughter, we'll happily slope.
To realms far away, where silliness reigns,
In a maze made of giggles and playful chains!

Beyond the Stilled Threshold

A door ajar with a creaky grin,
Unfolding tales where silliness spins.
Inviting whispers float through the crack,
Where gumball machines are lawfully back.

Old shoes dance like they own the night,
While ceiling fans buzz in sheer delight.
With pie on the ceiling and cats in hats,
The laughter blossoms, just like the spats.

To realms where the spaghetti grows on trees,
And polka-dotted elephants do as they please.
We gather the light with giggles and cheers,
Leaving behind all our worldly fears.

So let's dive deep through this whimsical door,
With sprinkles of joy to endlessly explore.
Hand in hand, as the fun spins unfurls,
We'll dance through the laughter of absurdities swirls!

www.ingramcontent.com/pod-product-compliance
Lightning Source LLC
Chambersburg PA
CBHW060139230426
43661CB00003B/484